In the Garden

Written by Marie Layson-Dale

Illustrated by Aurore Damant

The man taps.
Tap, tap, tap!

The cat can hear the man.

The cat hisses.
Hiss, hiss, hiss!

The bird can hear the cat.

The bird cheeps.
Cheep, cheep, cheep!

The man can hear the bird.